That's Another Story

BOOK FOUR

Paul Groves and Nigel Grimshaw
Illustrated by Martin Pitts

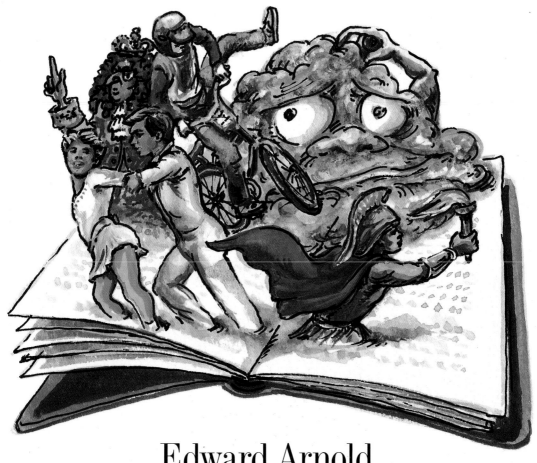

Edward Arnold

A division of Hodder & Stoughton

LONDON   MELBOURNE   AUCKLAND

Note to the Teacher

In reading level and in content, the material in this last book of the four book series is directed towards the upper forms of primary schools. The main concern, as the title suggests, has been with story-telling. The emphasis here, however, as in the third book, is more on the actual, although we have included fantasy stories and a poem which are intended to generate the children's own pieces of creative writing.

The first set of exercises following each passage asks for details from the text. The second set requires more thought and asks for inferences to be drawn. The third set incorporates some work on language skills, such as cloze, and opportunities for predictive and personal invention, along with group discussion.

As in the other books of the series, children will meet with characters in the reading passages with whom they can easily identify. The tone, where possible, continues to be light and humorous, although this last book, to reflect growing maturity, incorporates more fact.

© 1989 Paul Groves, Nigel Grimshaw, Martin Pitts

First published in Great Britain 1989

ISBN 0 7131 7764 0

Typeset in Linotron Optima by Rowland Phototypesetting Ltd, Bury St Edmunds, Suffolk
Printed and bound in Hong Kong for Edward Arnold, the educational, academic and medical publishing division of Hodder and Stoughton Ltd, Mill Road, Dunton Green, Sevenoaks, Kent by Colorcraft Ltd

Contents

1 The Tunnel

Alan and Claire ran for the school bus. They were almost late again. They clambered on and rushed down the aisle to find a seat. The bus was its usual noisy self with the children shouting and jumping up and down. Alan punched his friend Ali and sat down beside him. Ali gave him a sweet and a friendly dig in the ribs. Claire was soon in deep conversation with Alison about a project they were both doing on the village.

For Alan and Claire the journey was about three miles to the school in the town round twisty lanes. They got on at the last stopping point for the bus. Looking up, Claire just caught the face of the driver in the mirror; he was not Jack, the normal, ill-tempered driver, but an evil-looking man with a very big head and pointed ears. His grin in the mirror made Claire feel slightly uncomfortable, as if he were the kind of man her parents had always warned her about. But she said nothing to Alison.

Then it happened. They went under the railway bridge and they were suddenly in a tunnel. Claire knew it was a tunnel because it was like being on the Underground. Her ears popped and dark walls flashed by on either side, and the sound of the bus's engine bounced off them in a great roar. The shouting and play stopped. *There was no tunnel on the way to school.* Claire's whole body felt numb and under the noises of the tunnel a repetitive tune played in her head as if from a far-off synthesiser. Then she felt as if her mind were being drilled and this was followed by a great flash of purple light. Laughing suddenly started again. Claire opened her eyes. The bus was back on the road to school; there was the council estate.

The children got off the bus at school. No one said anything at all about the tunnel. Claire wanted to, but in a strange way she could not find the words to explain her experience. She ran from one child to the next. She could tell from the look in their eyes that they had had the same experience, but not one of them could talk about it.

Read it again

1   How do we know Alan and Claire are late before the story says so?

2   How far was their journey?

3   What project are Claire and Alison doing?

4   What is odd about the driver?

5   How did Claire know it was a tunnel?

6   Why did the shouting and the playing stop?

7   What 'played' in Claire's head?

8   What happened at the end of the tunnel?

9   How did Claire know that all the children had had the same experience?

Think it out – talk or write

1 Why might Claire and Alan have been late?

2 Why do you sometimes punch a friend?

3 What part might the strange driver play in the story?

4 Where might he be from?

5 What might the tunnel be?

6 What might the repetitive tune be?

7 Where might the purple light come from?

8 Why might the children not be able to talk about their frightening experience?

Write now

Use your answers to 'Think it out' 3–8 to work out an explanation for the story. Or continue the story . . .

2 The Marathon

Over 2,000 years ago, the Persians invaded Greece. Outnumbered, the Greeks fought them at a place called Marathon. The people of Athens waited, fearing what would happen. When the Greeks won the battle, a runner, Phaedipides, ran over 20 miles to bring the good news. He had already taken part in the battle. He was then sent on a further 200 miles to Sparta to tell the news there. On arrival he collapsed and died.

That, at least, is the story. The first modern Olympic marathon was run in 1896, when the first modern Olympic Games were held. That marathon was run over 40 kilometres, or 24 miles, 1,504 yards. It was run from Marathon to Athens and the winner was a Greek.

Nowadays, a modern marathon is run over 26 miles, 385 yards. This was the distance run in 1908 when the Olympic Games were held in Britain. The course was from Windsor Castle to the White City Stadium in London. That distance was exactly 26 miles. The 385 yards were added to make the race finish exactly in front of the royal box in the stadium.

At the Fourth Olympic Games, Oxo provided refreshments for the marathon runners. These included hot and cold Oxo, bananas and rice pudding, and Oxo and soda water.

Recently, 'fun runs' or marathons for everybody have become popular. In the London marathon in 1986, over 19,000 took part. This included wheelchair athletes as well. One in ten of the competitors was a woman.

Whether you're a world-class athlete or a fun runner, the problems of the marathon are the same. Feet get sore and you may get blisters. Cramp is a great problem. Sweating takes all the water out of a person's body. So, while you race you must drink. At about 18 to 22 miles, you 'hit the wall'. By that time the body has used up all its normal energy. After that you start drawing energy from body fat. This can cause you to feel dizzy and stagger. Eating more carbohydrates, called carbo-loading, three days before the race helps to overcome this. A fun runner can take four to five hours to complete a marathon. A world-class athlete can do it in just over two hours. That means running something like a five minute mile for mile after mile.

In 1984 the first woman's marathon was held in the Olympic Games in Los Angeles. The winner was Joan Benoit. It took her 2 hours 21 minutes.

There is no world marathon record as each course is different. At the time of writing this book, the fastest time was that of Carlos Lopez who ran a marathon in Rotterdam in 2 hours, 7 minutes, 12 seconds at the age of 39.

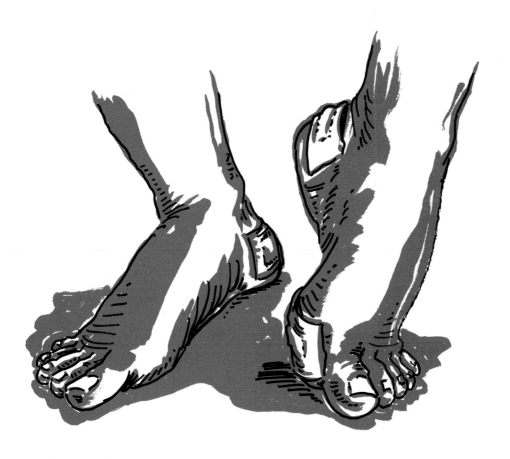

Read it again

1 Who fought in the battle of Marathon?

2 What happened to the runner who brought the news of the victory?

3 When was the first Olympic marathon held?

4 How long is the modern marathon?

5 Why is there an extra 385 yards?

6 How many ran in the London marathon of 1986?

7 Mention two problems of marathon running.

8 How can you help to overcome 'hitting the wall'?

9 What speed does a good runner average?

10 Who won the first woman's Olympic marathon?

Think it out – talk or write

1 Why do you think this race really hurts a runner?

2 Why do people take part in such a gruelling race for fun?

3 What should you do before you can run a marathon?

4 Why are some marathons harder than others?

5 What foods would you eat if you were carbo-loading?

6 Should all athletic events be open to women? Why?

7 People can now run races over distances of 100 kilometres. What is your opinion of this?

Copy this out and put in the missing words:

Marathon running has become very ————. The London marathon ———— thousands of runners. Many do it just for ————. Most runners suffer some ————. Blisters on the ———— are a big problem. You can also get ———— in the legs. At about ———— miles you 'hit the wall'. This means you have ———— up your ———— energy.

3 The Coming of the Monster

There is a deep gorge, a steep-sided valley, through the rocks in the hills above the village of Histington. People who know about rocks say it was formed in the Ice Age. But if you go there and talk to Mr Tufton, he will tell you a different story. He is a hundred years old. His face is wizened; he has a long grey beard and deep-set eyes. You will find him outside the pub on a sunny day. This is his story of the gorge.

Many years ago when the villagers were simple farmers, there was a terrible thunderstorm. When the skies had cleared they were amazed to see on top of the hill a great silver thing like a giant castle. Sitting by it was the ugliest creature they had ever seen. It was bigger than the tallest tree and covered in blue scales; it had red, fiery eyes the size of plates, three arms ending in huge claws and it smelt terribly.

The creature told the villagers it had come out of the sky from a land beyond the sun. It had been blown off course by a solar storm. In a huge voice it demanded food.

Within three days, it had eaten all the bread in the village. It demanded more and said it would kill the villagers one by one if they did not get it. They found fruit and other things for it but these supplies only lasted three more days; they had nothing left and sat waiting in their cottages to be killed.

The monster trundled down the hill and knocked down the wall of the first cottage it came to. As the wall fell down, the creature found itself looking into a mirror. 'Who is that?' it demanded.

'That is you,' said the villagers.

'But I'm ugly. Is it really me?'

'Yes,' they told him.

The creature sat down and huge tears welled up in its eyes. Then it cried and great rivers fell down his cheeks. Soon there was a flood; this turned into a raging torrent down the hillside which tore away trees and rocks. Then the monster went back to its strange machine and flew away.

'That was how the gorge was formed,' says Mr Tufton.

Read it again

1　When do people say that the gorge was formed?

2　What did Mr Tufton say formed it?

3　Describe two ways in which the creature was ugly.

4　Mention two things to show it was big.

5　Where had the creature come from?

6　Why had it come to Earth?

7　How quickly did it eat all the bread in the village?

8　What did it threaten to do then?

9　Why couldn't it carry out that threat?

10　What did it do when it saw itself in the mirror?

Think it out – talk or write

1 What is a gorge?

2 Give one reason why you doubt Mr Tufton's story.

3 What would be the modern name for 'the great silver thing like a giant castle'?

4 What evidence is there that (a) the creature had never seen itself before (b) it must have lived alone all its life?

5 Which reason would you like to believe for the way the gorge was formed? Say why.

6 What causes rocks to be shaped in different forms?

7 Make up another title for the story.

8 Why are creatures in space stories usually ugly?

Show that you know the meaning of the following words by putting each one in a sentence of your own:

wizened, amazed, fiery, solar, welled up

4 Snow in the Country

'Cold!' say the old, watching the slow snow fall
And drivers curse it as their back wheels slide
But I don't mind those slanting flakes at all.
It's not the sledging down a fast hillside

Or snowball fights or snowmen. It's the way
Snow changes things. It caps a shabby line
Of brussel sprouts with frozen foam. By day –
Get close enough – you'll see its diamonds shine;

Step back and see its shadows, blue not grey.
At night, it's lit up with an inner glow
And fields and fields, all gleaming, stretch away.
It doesn't look the same in towns, I know,

But I don't live in town and I can trace
Bird track or small paw track cut in the bright
Crisp sweep, while wind drives snow specks in my face,
Crunching my own track in the pure, dry white.

It's inconvenient and it's cold. It's wet.
It holds up traffic – all of this I know.
I don't deny it. I agree. And yet –
There's something rather splendid about snow.

Read it again

1 How do the old react to snow?

2 What do drivers do?

3 What can you do on a fast hillside?

4 How else does the poem say you can play in the snow?

5 What does snow look like on the sprouts?

6 Where does the writer of the poem live?

7 What tracks does the writer see in the snow?

8 Mention one reason why snow is inconvenient.

9 How does the poet sum up his feelings about snow?

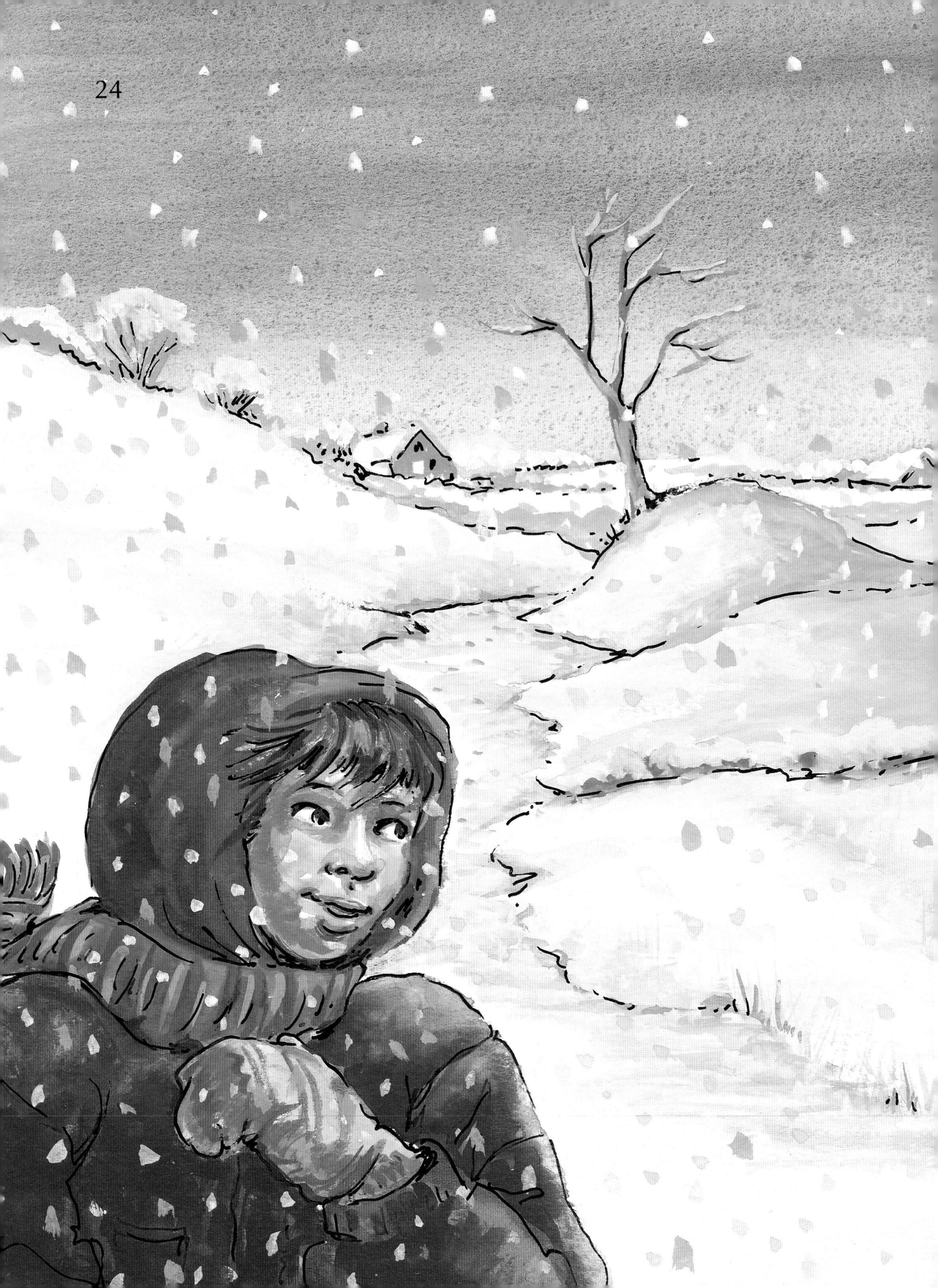

Think it out – talk or write

1 In what ways does snow affect old people? You can mention some that are not in the poem.

2 Why might snowflakes 'slant'?

3 Why does the poet really like snow?

4 Why are the brussel sprouts 'shabby'?

5 Why does snow 'shine'?

6 Why might snow not be the same in towns as in the countryside?

7 Why does the poet call snow 'dry white'?

8 In what ways is snow inconvenient to traffic?

Describe in a few sentences:

1 What it is like to walk in heavy snow.

2 How it feels to have snow driven into your face by the wind.

3 What it is like to build a snowman.

5 Which Came First — the Chicken or the Egg?

Once there was a mean king who had a big library. It was the biggest library in the world. He sent men all round the country to buy books for it. He spent all his money on books and very little on his family.

He read from dawn till dusk but he was not satisfied. He was not satisfied because his books could not tell him which came first, the chicken or the egg.

Then one day a dwarf came to his court. 'I hear you collect books,' he said. 'I can write you a book that will tell you anything you want to know.'

The king's eyes lit up. 'Anything?'

'Yes, anything. But you must keep me for seven years. I must work in private and not be disturbed.'

The king agreed. For the first few years he fed the dwarf well, much better than his own family. Then he began to wonder if the dwarf was tricking him. When he asked questions at the dwarf's door he got no reply. So he began to send in worse food. In the end he was only sending in bread and water.

At last came the day. The king waited at the door. The door opened. Out staggered the dwarf carrying a book three times his own size. He was so thin you could see his skull through his skin.

The king seized the book and opened it at the first page.
'Why!' he raged. 'It's in a strange language!'
'It's the old language of the dwarfs,' said the dwarf. 'I am the only one left in the world who can understand it.'
'Then translate it at once,' said the king.
'I am too weak from lack of food,' said the dwarf.
'Bring the finest meal in the court,' ordered the king.
The dwarf ate the meal. It took a long time. The king got impatient. Then the dwarf began: 'Once upon a time . . .' Then he fell down dead.

The king sent men all over the world to try and find someone who could translate the dwarf's book. They found no one. The king got into such a rage he died.

All his books were sold to feed his family. Someone bought the dwarf's book. It could be in a library near you. If you can find it, it will tell you which came first — the chicken or the egg. If you can read the dwarf's language.

Read it again

1 How big was the library?

2 How long did the king read each day?

3 What question did he want the answer to?

4 How did the dwarf want to work?

5 How well did the king feed the dwarf?

6 In what language was the book written?

7 What happened when the dwarf began to translate?

8 Why did the king die?

Think it out – talk or write

There are some parts of the story we do not know because we are not told about them. Can you invent them?

1 How old was the king?

2 Where was his country?

3 In what building did he live?

4 Who was in his family?

5 In what other ways than food could he be mean?

6 How tall was the dwarf? Describe him.

7 Where did he come from?

8 What did the dwarf do in the room? Did he write all the time?

9 Where could the dwarf have got such a large book to write in?

10 Where did the ink come from?

11 Write some of the strange language of the dwarf. It could be a picture language.

Discuss in small groups

1 What does the story teach you?

2 What question would you most like answered?

3 What book would you most like to find?

6 Program Bug

One day Gita made up a computer program. It was to sort two words into alphabetical order. This was the program:

```
100   REM**FIRST IN ALPHA-ORDER**
110   INPUT 'FIRST NAME'; A$
120   INPUT 'SECOND NAME'; B$
130   IF A$ < B$ THEN 160
140   PRINT 'FIRST IN ALPHA-ORDER IS ';B$
150   GOTO 170
160   PRINT 'FIRST IN ALPHA-ORDER IS';A$
170 END
```

She thought that she would run the program by putting in the names of her pets. She had a dog: Tom. And she had a cat: Mac. She ran the program:

```
RUN
FIRST NAME ? TOM
SECOND NAME ? MAC
FIRST IN ALPHA-ORDER IS TOM
```

That was wrong. It should have been Mac. Gita looked for the
bugs in the program. She could find none. It kept printing TOM.

A feeling came over her that Tom was in danger. She ran out
into the street and called his name. A bark came from a long
way off. It was Tom's bark. It was coming from the canal.

She ran to the canal as quickly as she could. There was Tom in the middle on a piece of ice. 'Hold on, Tom!' she called. She ran along the bank. A window cleaner was coming along. She asked for help.

The window cleaner pushed out his ladder on to the ice. Tom ran across it. He was safe.

Gita went back home and ran the program again:

```
RUN
FIRST NAME ? TOM
SECOND NAME ? MAC
FIRST IN ALPHA-ORDER IS MAC
```

Gita told her Mum and Dad. 'We don't understand computers,' they told her. Gita did not understand either.

Read it again

1 Give two meanings of the word 'Bug'.

2 What strange thing happened when Gita first ran the program?

3 Why was it strange?

4 What made her think that Tom was in danger?

5 Where did the bark come from?

6 Why was it a good thing that she met the window cleaner?

7 What happened when she ran the program again after the rescue?

8 Why did Gita not understand what had happened to the program?

Think it over – talk or write

1 Which is right:
  I bought a program of the teams at the football match.
  I bought a programme of the teams at the football match.

2 In what ways have you used a computer?

3 Make up another title for the story.

4 How does this story make computers seem strange?

5 Is there any danger of people relying on computers?

6 What has been the attitude of your parents to computers?

Copy this out and put in the missing words:

Gita took her program to ————. The teacher said, 'Put it in the
————'. 'Well done, ————' said the teacher when she ————
the program ————.
  'But it did not ————, at first,' said ————.
  'You must have been ————,' said the teacher.
  'No, it was ———— about Tom,' ———— Gita.

7 The Experiment

An American scientist wanted to find out if girls were born knowing how to be mothers or whether they had to learn it. He could not experiment with humans so he took some monkeys away from their mothers at birth. He put them in a cage with two wire-mesh model monkeys. One model monkey was all bare wire but contained a feeding nipple for milk; the other model had no feeding nipple but was covered in a soft cloth.

The baby monkeys would only spend feeding time on the bare wire monkey; the rest of the time would be spent on or near the cloth-covered monkey. If danger threatened, and the scientist frightened them with a toy soldier which played a drum, they would go straight to the cloth-covered monkey and cling on.

When later these monkeys were mated and became mothers they had no idea how to bring up their babies. They took little notice of them. One even put her hand on her baby's head and leant heavily on it.

The scientist felt that he had proved his point that you have to be properly mothered to learn to be a mother yourself.

The fondness for the cloth mother also showed how important it is to cuddle a baby softly.

Read it again

1   What country did the scientist come from?

2   What did he want to find out?

3   What did he do?

4   What was the first kind of model monkey like?

5   What was the second kind like?

6   Which model did the monkeys like best?

7   What did he use the toy soldier for?

8   What happened when the monkeys in the experiment became mothers themselves?

9   What did the scientist think he had proved?

10 Why did he think cuddling a baby was important?

Think it over – talk or write

1 Why could the scientist not experiment with humans?

2 How do you feel about him experimenting on monkeys in this way?

3 What seems more important than food to young creatures?

4 Why might the mated mothers have no idea how to bring up their babies?

5 What does a baby know how to do without the help of its mother?

6 Which of these experiments would you not allow on animals:
skin testing for cosmetics
drug injections to test drugs intended for humans
learning experiments like the one above.
Give reasons for each answer.

Copy this out and put in the missing words:

This is about an ——— scientist who ——— on monkeys. He wanted to see how they ——— up without their ———. He made wire models: one was of ——— wire; the other was covered in a soft ———. The baby monkeys ——— the cloth model.

8 The Silliest Story of All Time

I want to tell you about the silliest story of all time. It's called 'Goldilocks and the Three Bears'. There's this kid, Goldilocks; not Jane or Dawn or some normal name. But she's got this long blonde hair she flaunts down her back so she calls herself by it which is nutty. She's a real smarty and yukky and her nose never runs or nothing like some real kid.

It seems one day she's in the woods alone. Now, no self-respecting parents would ever let a kid wander off alone and if she did you'd have all the Fuzz in creation looking for her.

She comes to a little house. She goes inside, which is breaking and entering or some such crime which you wouldn't expect this kind of high-class kid to do. Inside, she finds three chairs: a big chair, a medium size chair, and a teeny-weeny chair. Being dumb, she puts her great strapping body in the teeny-weeny chair and breaks it.

Then she sees three bowls of porridge on the table. She tastes the biggest bowl which is bad manners of the first order. I mean, to mess about with someone else's food! Then she licks the spoon of the medium size bowl. Quite disgusting! Both these bowls of porridge are too hot for her so she samples the teeny-weeny bowl and wolfs it down because it is cool. It's about the only cool thing in this story.

Having had a bellyful of porridge, she feels sleepy which is daft because it is breakfast time and we presume she's had a full night's sleep. She finds three beds of the same three sizes as the chairs, etc. and of course, even though her legs flop over the end, she chooses the teeny-weeny bed.

Well, it seems that this cottage belongs to three bears, though any fool knows that bears live in caves. They've left their porridge to cool while they've gone for a walk. As porridge is eaten in winter these three bears should be hibernating, but they're too dumb to know it.

They come home and go through some patter about 'Who's been sitting in my chair?' which is crazy because (a) bears don't talk and (b) how the hell do you tell if someone's been sitting in a wooden chair? They go through the same routine about the porridge and the teeny-weeny bear loses his cool when he finds all his has been scoffed. Then he goes bananas when he finds this yukky girl in his bed asleep.

Now, this is supposed to wake her up and she runs away. I mean how could she escape from three grizzlies in a small room? They should have boffed her and made her into a stew with the porridge, as they seem to have cooking facilities. That would have made a better story.

Read it again

1 What is the silliest story of all time according to the writer?

2 Who is the heroine of it?

3 What does the writer think a real kid would be like?

4 Why is the writer critical of Goldilocks being alone?

5 What does Goldilocks do first?

6 What does she do next?

7 Which bed did Goldilocks choose?

8 Why does the writer mention winter?

9 What does the writer say bears don't do?

10 How does the writer want the story to end?

Think it out – talk or write

1   What are the main reasons why the writer finds the story silly?

2   What is your opinion of the story? Did you like it as a young child?

3   When do you first know that this is a funny account of the story of Goldilocks?

4   Give two examples of slang.

5   What do you think about talking animals in stories? Do you grow out of them as you get older or is there a place for them? What about cartoons, for instance?

6   What does 'loses his cool' mean?

7   What is 'patter'?

8   What do you think of the writer's suggested ending?

Copy this out and put in the missing words:

In this story the writer makes ——— of 'Goldilocks and the Three Bears'. He describes her as a ———. He makes her going into the ——— seem like a ———. When she eats the ——— the writer says it is ———. He would like the story to end by Goldilocks being ——— into a ———.

9 Tristan's Race

The cups and the trophies on the shelf in Tristan's bedroom showed he was the best junior BMX rider in his area. But he was now on the way to Slough for his first really big race.

As soon as he and his Dad arrived they unloaded the precious bike carefully. It was Tristan's third. The first two had been broken in crashes. This one was much stronger. It had cost £400. But some of Tristan's 15 opponents had two bikes and one small, tough-looking lad had three. He was trying them out, deciding which was best suited for this course.

'They're works riders. They're sponsored by the BMX factory,' explained Tristan's Dad. 'Don't worry,' he added, 'they can only ride one bike at once.'

Tristan smiled. But he was scared. What had he let himself in for? There were three American boys talking together. They looked very confident. Tristan's Dad had noticed them too.

'Well, they said it was an international event, so what do you expect? Anyway, these Americans are not what they are cracked up to be.'

Tristan knew his Dad was trying to cheer him up. BMX racing had been popular in America for years. Their riders were very good. When the eight riders lined up for the first heat, Tristan forgot about his fears. He was next to a very big boy with a red face. You could hardly see his bike when he sat on it. 'At least I can beat him,' thought Tristan. 'He's too big for a BMX.'

But he was wrong. It was the hardest race Tristan had been in. Going into the big jump half way round the circuit, Tristan was sixth — only four qualified for the final. Tristan gritted his teeth and took off with plenty of height to clear the jump — and just enough to clear the bodies and bikes of two riders tangled in a heap on the other side.

Now Tristan was fourth, and he stayed there till the end, just qualifying for the final.

Tristan's Dad was pleased. 'Best you've ever done,' he said. 'But that big lad is good.'

The big boy won easily. It just showed you how you could be fooled by appearances.

'Riders ready! Pedals ready! Go!' said the starter, and off went Tristan and seven others in the final.

First corner, water-jump, triple and round the second corner with Tristan third. He could hardly believe it. Where were the Americans and the works bikes kids? One was in front – just behind the big boy – but Tristan was beating the rest. Tristan clung on. He was good at corners and just held his own in the straight. Down went the kid in front, sliding painful yards along the gravel, his helmet bumping against a stone. The last big jump – a triple – three solid bumps at least three feet high. If Tristan could take them in one, he would fly past the big boy in the air. Up went Tristan. He had a quick sight of the big boy about to take the third jump and then all went dark.

Tristan woke up in the ambulance.

'You did brilliantly,' said his Dad. 'If you hadn't come off you'd have won.'

'I will next time,' said Tristan, and winced as the ambulance man treated his leg.

Read it again

1 Where was the big BMX race?

2 How many bikes had Tristan had?

3 How many were in the race?

4 How did Tristan feel before the race?

5 How did Tristan manage to qualify for the final after lying sixth in the heat?

6 Who won that heat?

7 How many riders were in the final?

8 What position is Tristan in round the second corner of the final?

9 What was the last jump?

10 What damage did Tristan do to himself?

Think it out – talk or write

1 What does sponsored mean?

2 Why do you feel that Tristan has not much of a chance?

3 What result did you expect in the final?

4 Why is it harder to race if you are overweight?

5 What sports can large people be good at?

6 Why are you not told who won?

Copy this out and put in the missing words:

If you are ——— about sport you want to make it sound ———.
In this story a boy gets into the ——— of a BMX race. He is
——— coming to the last jumps. He tries to ——— off into the
air to ——— them all. The next thing he ——— he wakes up in
the ———.

10 The Torvill and Dean Ice Tent

Over 10,000 yards of special, reinforced, flame-proof PVC material are used in the construction of the Big Top. The overall length of the tent is 330 feet and the width 222 feet. The construction itself is larger than the size of a football pitch and is the largest known tent in the world.

The Torvill and Dean World Tour Big Top was made in the tiny village of Tauranga in New Zealand.

It took over 9 months to build and the workforce of sail-makers, engineers and canvas workers numbered 50 people. Three hundred and seventy-eight poles, including the 8 massive king poles standing 80 feet high, keep the structure aloft.

Over 10 miles of steel cable have been used in the construction. Thirty-six miles of timber planking forms the basis of the seating gallery which holds 6,996 chairs.

Two hundred and fifty 10 feet long steel tent pegs anchor the structure firmly to the ground.

At the rear of the tent is a mini city of dressing rooms, work shops, wardrobe facilities and offices.

A staff exceeding 150 people is required for each performance. The portable ice floor covers an area of 11,000 sq ft and is the largest portable ice floor in the world.

The ice itself is 4 inches thick.

It takes three days from the time the giant refrigeration plant is switched on to achieve ice suitable for the Torvill and Dean World Tour Company to work on. The refrigeration plant requires a semi-trailer to transport it from place to place and is capable of making an ice floor outdoors in the extreme conditions of the tropics.

The lighting rig is one of the biggest ever used in a theatrical presentation. Over 450 lamps provide a myriad of dazzling effects.

The massive sound system is the most advanced of its type employing the latest international technology.

Read it again

1 How much material was used to make the tent?

2 Where was it made?

3 How many people made it?

4 How many does it hold?

5 What is at the rear of the tent?

6 How many staff are required at each performance?

7 How big is the ice floor?

8 How long does it take to refrigerate the ice?

9 How many lamps are there in the lighting system?

10 What is special about the sound system?

Think it out – talk or write

1 Why would the ice tent be difficult to move from place to place?

2 What might the king poles be?

3 What might the main problems be in making a tent so big?

4 Why would the tickets to the show be expensive?

5 What is a 'lighting rig'?

6 What is the best show you have ever seen?

Show that you know the meaning of these words by using each one in a sentence of your own:

reinforced, construction, structure, facilities, extreme, presentation, myriad, international, technology